LOVE UNBOUND
JOSEPH R. ADOMAVICIA

"Love Unbound"
Written and arranged by Joseph R. Adomavicia
All rights reserved.

Contents

8. Love Unbound
9. One Of A Kind
11. When I Look At You
12. Lost In The Stars
13. If There Is Ever
14. My Love, For You
15. Swimming Through My Soul
16. Alive Again
17. Woman Of My Dreams
18. Seamless
19. My World
20. Her Heart, My Heart
21. Sunflower Girl
22. Safe And Secure
23. All That Is True Lies In You
24. The Stage Is Set, The Word Is Yours
25. California Sunshine
26. The House That Love Built
27. All That Ever Was And All That Ever Is
28. Romanticized Intricacies
29. Ride Or Die
30. Love's Taste
31. Soul Searching
32. In The Name Of Love And Metaphor
33. The Very Best And Very Worst
34. Lean Back Into My Arms
35. Something Clever, But Nothing Cliché
36. A Whole New Entirety
37. Solemn Truth
38. Held Within The Sun
40. Suppose I Said
41. It's In Every Little Thing You Do
42. If I Was, Shall You Be
43. I See You At The Day's Edge
44. Light Of My Love
45. Love's Purpose
46. Beauty In Tragedy
47. Luscious Love
48. Reason To Smile
49. Let It Fly
50. I Can See The Beauty
51. My Gem, She Shines, Oh Yes, She Does
52. Straight From The Heart

53. Love's Sight
54. You And I Must Be
55. Elegant Continuity
56. The Doors Of My Soul
57. Prominence
58. The Presence Of Her Excellence
59. Your Love Is My Faith
60. Without You
61. Beauty's Becoming (The Love We Share)
62. Soul On Fire
63. I'm At My Happiest When I'm With You
64. Roses In The Garden
65. The Key To My Serenity
66. Mutual Fate In Oceans of Love
67. Fearless (Love Hard Or Not At All)
68. Looking At You
69. My Last Sheet Of Paper

LOVE UNBOUND

With every day passing

we grow,

our love,

grows.

And we become the flower

under our sunshine.

Rainy days make way

giving life to love,

our own

blossoming

for all to see.

A.L.P

JOE ADOMAVICIA

Edited by, T.J. Burlee

Graphic Design and typesetting Mitch Green

LOVE UNBOUND

Love is a living lie to those who fear it.

Love Unbound

Lead me to a land where love is unbound
and only songs of harmony are profound.
In due time, circumstance, cold as space,
will tear the flesh of love,
leaving it to bleed like a sieve.
And when its cries ring out into the open,
at least then the vastness of its depths
will have awoken.
If love's consequence brings forth the worst,
then in reciprocity above what is bleak,
it will bring the best just as well.

There must be a land
where love is unbound.

One Of A Kind

It's quarter to one
and you're all that's on my mind.
You're my girl,
you're my love,
and you're one of a kind.
And come quarter to six
when my eyes open
and it's time to go to work,
it's accurate to say that
until you're in my arms again,
my day will not be complete.
No other love I ever thought true
could ever compete with the love you've bestowed upon me.
Some measure love with time,
but, what I've come to find
is that no matter
if it's in two months time
or two years time
the love we've contrived
will only become more refined
within our definition.

It's now quarter to two
and you're all that's on my mind.
You're my girl,
you're my love,
and you're one of a kind.
I lay awake wrapped in a quilt that smells like you
and although my eyes are heavy,
still I write steadily
of my feelings of love
in the name of you.
My mind knows no limit
on the words it must exhibit,
and by quarter to three
my dreams will be exquisite,
because I will fall asleep to my thoughts of you.
When you wake
let there be no doubt in the truth

that my days spent with you
are the best of all,
for,
you're my girl,
you're my love,
and you're one of a kind.
I love you.

When I Look At You

You are the best part of my day.
No, really,
you can roll and cross your eyes
and laugh like you always do,
but you are so damn beautiful;
inside and out.
And truly, when I look at you,
I see the past,
and see what my life
has been missing.
When I look at you,
I see the present,
and get lost in your presence;
there is not a worry in the world
when I am amidst your elegance.
When I look at you,
I can see the future
in you and I,
and it isn't just me,
the world sees it and feels it too.
I can hear the birds
whistle, sing, rustle, and bustle
through the leaves
to take flight in harmony
of you and I.

Lost In The Stars

It was just about midnight
when my love and I
sat and burned a smoke away.
As our eyes rose into
the ebony skies
we began counting stars,
and, to me,
there was nothing more romantic than that.
We would be there forever
counting on one another
to count countless stars
with no one except one another.

If There Is Ever

If there is ever a moment
you don't feel beautiful,
tell me. I'll remind you of
how much I adore every
inch of your existence.

If there is ever a moment,
you feel alone, call my name.
I'll be on my way to fill the void
with smiles, love, and laughter,
or even a silent companion;
a shoulder to rest your head upon.

If there is ever a moment,
your heart feels broken,
no need to call the doctor;
I'll be the one to tend
to your wounds,
kiss it, and make it all better.

If there is ever a moment,
your soul feels lost,
please, don't worry;
the best part of being soul mates is there
will always be a piece of you
inside of me.

JOE ADOMAVICIA

My Love, For You

The sun shines
as the love in my heart
shines for you
and the ocean's hues of blue
inhale and exhale
as my words of love
transfer from seeds of thought,
to words blossoming into poems that flourish,
telling stories of two hearts in harmony
in celebration of their existence.
And in that instance
substance is of abundance—
my love, for you.

Swimming Through My Soul

The seven seas
could separate You and I,
but, it could never hold testament
to the unity we have contrived.
And if I met my death
before your presence
is bestowed upon me again—
my last breath
would be in the name of you.
Inherit my spirit and carry on,
for, the seven seas could separate
You and I,
but, it could never drown out
the thoughts of you
that stream through my mind
or the pieces of you
that swim through my soul.

Alive Again

I feel alive again,
within your words
and within your skin's texture.
Our chemistry
is quite the pleasant mixture.
Destiny is enamored,
painting our picture.

I feel alive again,
within your clever jokes
and those Camel Crush cigs you smoke.
You drive and we sing along to songs
that connect our hearts
as two people who aren't afraid
of the world's woes.

I feel alive again,
within the light strokes
of the sea in your eyes,
and within your free-spirited charisma.
You walk through the fields of my mind
with a daisy in your hair
as a form of assurance,
conducive to which we are becoming.

I feel alive again,
within the potential
blooming in you and I.
And now,
finally,
I feel alive again.

Woman Of My Dreams

My aim is not to find
the woman of my dreams,
but it is to find she who
urges me to dream,
and dreams alongside me.

My aim is not to find
the woman of my dreams,
but it is to find she who
can silence my screams
when nightmares
take hold of my dreams.

My aim is not to find
the woman of my dreams
but it is to find she who
is both the complement
and supplement
to my geometry.

My aim is not to find
the woman of my dreams
but it is to find she who
sees me as I see her,
nothing more nothing less,
two hearts concur,
beating as one
bar none.

Seamless

We are seamless, you and I.
We are the beauty in poetry,
in subtle simplicity.
Extraneous distractions
are meaningless infractions
upon the image of the forthcoming.
What was and what is to be
is nothing other than destiny.
Do not dwell on what has passed us by,
we are seamless, you and I.
We are the beauty in poetry,
in subtle simplicity.
Life's novelties come and go,
but if there is one thing to know
about what has come and what must go,
it is to understand that to find a true realization
of one self and in another
is to create love's fluency.

My World

With all the women in the world
she found me,
just as I found her.
Both of us,
searching for security,
searching for serenity
in the confines of another person,
in a world hellbent for calamity.
And this, and this alone
keeps me going in a world
where loneliness grows
like moss on a mountainside.

JOE ADOMAVICIA

Her Heart, My Heart

Her heart, it beats,
my heart, it beats,
not in the name of me
but, in the name
of all that is to come.
What is nothing to some,
is everything to another.

Her heart, it beats,
my heart, it beats.
I feel them both
as we rest in each other's arms.
A steady, rhythmic beat,
and now our fervor,
our creation,
has ignited.

Her heart, it beats,
my heart, it beats,
life would be nothing
if not for the love we're offering.
Even if our hearts ceased to beat
the love we've pronounced
amounts to all we've lived for.

Her heart, it beats,
my heart, it beats,
her heart and my heart
beat as one,
in the name of all that is to come.

Sunflower Girl

You're my sunflower girl,
the way you twirl your curls,
move your hips,
sing, dance, and play
makes me wild,
wild like a heart untamed.
Your free spirit's merit
I'll inherit and share it.
O' and lest I forget those eyes,
a pair of eyes blue
like the waters of Bora Bora.
I'd swim in your ocean
and get lost
in the depths of your embodiment.
You're my sunflower girl,
you give joy to what isn't joyful.

Safe And Secure

I wonder if she knows
how safe and secure
she makes me feel.
It may seem trivial to you,
but for me, it is knowing,
that even at my worst
she will be at her best;
And what else could one ask for?
I have love and companionship
through all of the shades
this man could be.

All That Is True Lies In You

I'm not sure what it is yet,
and I can't quite put my finger on it,
but, maybe, it is in the sparkle in your eye,
or the way you talk to me
as if you have always known me.

I'm not sure what it is yet,
and I can't quite put my finger on it,
but, maybe, it is in the softness of your touch,
or the way you kiss me just underneath my chin
as if you could taste my love for you on my skin.

I'm not sure what it is yet,
and I can't quite put my finger on it,
but, maybe, it is in the serenity of your aura,
or the way you give me reason to smile
as if all you ever wanted was for me to live a life worthwhile.

I'm not sure what it is yet,
and I can't quite put my finger on it,
but, maybe, it is in the way you sing,
or the way you soothe my wounds,
as if all that was ever true, lies in you.

The Stage Is Set, The Word Is Yours

Please do tell me if I am wrong,
but there is this feeling in my gut so strong.
And you know if I speak to you in verse
with cadence of a song,
that you had my heart all along.
When we are in each other's presence
do you not feel as if you belong?
A feeling such as this can't be dismissed.
Please do tell me if I am wrong,
so I don't go putting my heart
where it doesn't belong,
and if it hurts then it hurts
I'd rather not live that lie
because even with a solid alibi
there isn't a lie worth telling
if it meant you dispelling
all of who you lead me to believe you are.
So please do tell me if I am wrong,
the stage is set, the word is yours.

California Sunshine

All mine, oh yes, you're all mine,
California sunshine
I tell ya, you're all mine.
You come and you go
but everyone knows
you're all mine
rain or shine
time after time
and time again.
I have felt your warmth
upon my face;
I have heard your words
of golden ecstasy
setting my whole soul into place
within the presence of your grace.

All mine, oh yes, you're all mine,
California sunshine
I tell ya, you're all mine.
You come and you go
but everyone knows
you're all mine
rain or shine
time after time
and time again.
It is only you who could do
this to me, you see,
and the only way for me
to be at ease
is to live out the love
of desire's necessities,
For, only you,
California sunshine,
deserve the best of me.

JOE ADOMAVICIA

The House That Love Built

Comfort bestowed as two hearts touch.
Find homage in my arms,
hold tight, and don't fret.
A set of watchful eyes,
fists, and an iron will
cast upon the brave soul who would try
to separate our love.
May our love remain resilient,
for, futility is not a possibility,
and so dare I say,
let us take pride and provide
integrity for the house that love built.

All That Ever Was And All That Ever Is

If all that ever was
comes 'round
to all that ever is,
then all I've ever been
in this life or another
has all been for you,
and if all that ever was
comes 'round
to all that ever is,
then all you've ever been
in this life or another
has all been for me.
By the hands of destiny
this propensity was crafted
becoming our purpose
for eternity.

Romanticized Intricacies

I will remember
how your index finger
traced calloused creases
intersecting on my palm
as if you were a seer
peering into my soul
searching for delicacies
unbeknownst to me.

I will remember
your soft and gentle touch,
swift like an October breeze
passing through me with ease,
carrying me along like leaves
rolling down a road destiny manifested.

I will remember
the way words fell from your lips
like songs of a seraph
bathed in a golden aura,
an illumination of hope
in a storm-cloud setting.

I will remember
currents of trust
streaming ever strong,
and towers of dependability
perpetuating romanticized intricacies
all in which I have shared with you.

Ride Or Die

She's my ride or die,
whatever I'd do for her
she'd do for me.
I'm her king,
she's my queen,
we're livin' and spreadin'
our love like it's magic
Disney has never seen.

She's my ride or die,
whatever she'd do for me
I'd do for her.
She's my queen,
I'm her king,
have you ever seen
romance so keen?
I'm tellin' ya it's the kind
that makes you
want to dance and sing.

She's my ride or die,
whatever I'd do for her
she'd do for me.
I'm her king,
she's my queen,
I'd rescue her from
the clutches of tragedy
for, when we found each other
she saved me
from my own travesty.

She's my ride or die,
whatever she'd do for me
she'd do for me.
I'm her king,
she's my queen,
there isn't any amount of
strife in this life
that will deter us from
livin' in and spreadin' our love.

Love's Taste

The beauty of getting to know someone,
is accepting them for their flaws, bright spots,
and everything in between, through the unseen.

The beauty of getting to know someone,
is accepting the fact you learn to love again
and leave behind the troubles of the past.

The beauty of getting to know someone,
is accepting the fact that vulnerabilities
and all possibilities are out in the open.

The beauty of getting to know someone,
is cherishing all of the special moments
and relishing love's taste in a new flavor.

The beauty of getting to know someone,
is cherishing a simple walk in the park,
and the moment when hands lace for the first time.

The beauty of getting to know someone,
is cherishing the fact some knows you
and will continue to cherish you as you do them.

Soul Searching

I, for one,
would rather search the ends of the earth
before I live and let time pass
with her soul left undiscovered.
If I cannot see love in another
how could I ever fathom it within myself?
And if I could not fathom it within myself,
would I not only be a shell of who I can truly be?
It is one thing to be broken
amongst shards of prior existence,
but to ignore the chance of resolve
through forgiveness
is the truth of pain
in constancy.

JOE ADOMAVICIA

In The Name Of Love And Metaphor

In the name of love and metaphor
I bring a rose not to say I love you,
because unconditionally
I would say it 100 times over again—
but I bring a rose to pluck the petals
and watch them dance
their way to the ground
to reside beside our feet.
And, while my hands rest gently upon your cheeks,
I know by pressing my lips against the warmth of yours,
I would hear the sounds of our hearts pumping in unison
and I would feel your taste as I inhaled your embrace,
savoring most importantly—
the fact that we, as the flower and the petals,
of what once was and will be,
is willing to live and die,
fulfilling destiny
in the name of love and metaphor.

The Very Best And Very Worst

If only I were to meet
a woman
who spoke to me
in all her intensities
I would embrace
her propensity passionately
and cherish
the inferno writhing
from the deepest crevices
of her soul –
at least then
I would be able to understand
the very worst
and very best of her.

JOE ADOMAVICIA

Lean Back Into My Arms

Lean back into my arms,
the depths of my heart
have love enough
to fill yours.
If one is better than none,
and yet two is still too lonesome,
love enough for three,
and, at the end of the day,
my love and all I can be
will be for you.
And if you are she
who is meant for me,
revel in glee and I too, will
lean back into your arms,
for the depths of your heart
have love enough to fill mine.

Something Clever, But Nothing Cliché

I have been thinking
of something clever,
but nothing cliché.
A single rose or an orchid
simply would not do,
no, it would never be enough
to compliment your beauty.
But, maybe, if I sang a line,
even two, you would see
beyond my off-pitched voice
I only sing to fit your tune,
to see you smile brighter
than sunshine on the ocean.
I have been thinking of you
as more than a lover,
but nothing cliché.
To say Romeo and Juliet,
two star-crossed lovers,
would doom me
right from the start.
But, what if I offered
you my hand to dance
under a star-kissed sky,
Would you accept my offer?
I dance to match your step,
and would take your hand,
because there is no other
in heart or mind.

JOE ADOMAVICIA

A Whole New Entirety

There is poetry in the bands
around newlyweds fingers,
there is poetry within the words
that fall from lover's lips,
and within small gestures,
or unimaginably titanic gifts
of love and devotion,
but, there is nothing more poetic
than the soulful idea
of millions of people,
heart and mind, aura and psyche,
searching for that one connection
that will guide them into
interpersonal intimacy and ecstasy.
Losing their old self in streams of memory, locking in,
focusing on their entire purpose refined by their own
individuality until that one defining moment when
another person creates a spark, a current, electrifying
an undeniable connection that makes both whole again
within a whole new entirety.

Solemn Truth

We have been broken
for as long as I can remember,
but don't worry,
we can pick the pieces up together.
To walk through the inferno,
to resolve within the waters
that quench our thirst—
is the step we must take first.
Unknowing eyes stare,
judgmental
within their misunderstanding.
And this is okay,
we don't need them to because
we understand one another,
and this lone, solemn truth
is the foundation of what our love can be.

Held Within The Sun

Just in case you are wondering
if I am like all those other men,
my dear, you are mistaken,
my love is yours for the taking.

I will not tell you
what you want to hear
but, what you need to hear,
and in the face of adversity,
whether it be sweet or sour,
I will speak of truths without fear.

Just in case you are wondering
if I am like all those other men,
my dear, you are mistaken,
my love is yours for the taking.

I would rather
let my actions speak
to you in ways my words
cannot, holding meaning,
far beyond the glittered horizon
in which, it be, held within the sun.

Just in case you are wondering
if I am like all those other men,
my dear, you are mistaken,
my love is yours for the taking.

I will not tell you
what you want to hear
but, what you need to hear,
saying the sky is blue year-round
when we know even the bluest sky
bares a hint of grey, but to take your
hand, withstanding the worst of the storm
would be proof enough to reassure you –
just in case you are wondering
if I am like all those other men,

LOVE UNBOUND

my dear, you are mistaken,
my love is yours for the taking.

Suppose I Said

Suppose I said the words written upon
the canvas of your soul were the same words
that filled the details of my own—
Would you believe me or
would it be safe to say
life brought us together in a
harmonious way?

Suppose I said the lone soldier sitting on
the shore was me, and you were the only
Passerby who crept by as the sun
receded below the ocean's edge—
Would you believe me or
would it be safe to say
life brought us together in a
harmonious way?

Suppose I said climbing the rustic trap rock ridges
of the Hanging Hills was only the beginning
of my willingness for you
on the path of your satisfaction—
Would you believe me or would it be safe to say
life brought us together in a
harmonious way?

Suppose I said the essence of existence
was within the air we breathe,
and we were one before
the thought could be conceived—
Would you believe me or
would it be safe to say
life brought us together in a
harmonious way?

It's In Every Little Thing You Do

It's in every little thing, you do,
and in every little thing, you say.
It's in the way you move,
that sets my heart
into a harmonic groove,
beating in the name of you.

The fact that I brought a smile to your face
is enough to make my day.
Some say it's just spring fever and hell
if they are right these feelings are the great deceiver,
but I refuse to live in fright.
Between you and I,
from where I see,
we are meant to be.

It's in every little thing, you do,
and in every little thing, you say.
It's in the way you move,
that sets my heart
into a harmonic groove,
beating in the name of you.

In this garden that is my love
there are flowers with
red and pink petals of passion and ecstasy
and in one brief moment
these petals begin to flow
amplifying an incomparable love
no other could compare.
This is how it feels when love is in our sight,
our electric delight.
Now tell me,
may we begin to live and love—
fearlessly,
fulfilling what is meant to be?

If I Was, Shall You Be

If I was the tectonic plates
holding our continent together—
shall you be the gift of life
sprouting from the fields of our unity?

If I was to become lost and fall apart,
would you guide my hands across
the Braille of your heart—
shall you be the guidance I have failed
to find within myself?

If I was the words of a poem
in which you could call home
shall you be the essence of a song
I have longed to listen to all along?

If I was the fluency
of love's rhetoric
or the light laughter of a limerick—
shall you be love personified
and form our story euphoric?

I See You At The Day's Edge

To hear your voice is to be kissed
by gentle undertones of a summer breeze,
to embrace your warmth
within the safety of my arms
sitting on the beach
treasuring your embrace.
I see you at the day's edge.
To gaze into your eyes
and realize your depth,
to delve into your moral compass
becoming inspired,
daring to travel and unravel
the mysteries of our worlds,
proves our love and admiration convened,
wholly and exclusively.
You are my serene setting—
I see you at the day's edge.

Light Of My Love

Light of my love;
lead me out of this slumber of darkness—
the caverns of my mind
a mural painted in deep hues of blue.
Light of my love;
return me to a time when I was stronger—
who other than you
would love me longer?
Light of my love;
it is you who has called out to me,
time after time—
and if loving you was a felony
I would serve the lengthiest crime.
Light of my love;
I can see the beauty,
I can feel the excellence of your presence.
I plead—light of my love,
when death prevails love me longer.

Love's Purpose

I have always wondered why
I can write about the ins and outs of love,
yet never find myself in love
outside of my words.
I suppose I am either
in tune with my muse
or at quarrel with the world—
worlds apart from reality.
Or maybe, simply,
I am enticed by the thought of love
unknowing of when its purpose will arrive.

Beauty In Tragedy

When I'm with you,
not only do I feel good about you,
but, I feel good about myself.
Like there was nothing ever wrong
with me to begin with.
These facts fill me with
one of the most satisfying feelings
about love and companionship
I've ever known.
Having you by my side
bares bare naked truth
of the beauty in tragedy.
In the present we have each other's presence to live for
and in the future, long after one of us is gone,
Our souls will remain two halves of the same being
Until there is nothing left to tell us any different.

Luscious Love

Oh my, oh my, luscious love stole my eye
take my hand and be free, join me, love me.
Life is but a journey not worth living
without you by my side, might you leave me
if my sails set sideward, might you stay if
our times reveled in smiles, beauty and love
so pure churning deep, in my beating heart.
The sun shall rise and the sun shall set and
what still remains, is that, our love, my dove,
is what propels us closer— two hearts that of
magnets to a ferrous metal—so close
beast nor harlot could tear our love apart.

Reason To Smile

Imagine an ample, open field.
Arms spread wide,
running, circling round
with a gorgeous, gracious smile
pearly whites, ear to ear, in fact.
O', what a day,
meant to be savored, relished and cherished.
Winds of old pass,
seemingly, right through you as
sparkling rays from a cloudless sky
shine on for miles and miles.
There is truth in facts,
that sometimes in life all we really need
is one breath of fresh air—
one cloudless summer day—
to rid us of a day's worries
reminding us that life isn't always bad,
and there is always a reason to smile.

Let It Fly

Staring out,
wondering when,
and hoping for.

Past,
present,
future disturbances,
let them go,
let them fly,
let destiny breed faith.

Feelings so true,
feeling so pure,
feelings so strong,
for so long.

Patience,
honesty,
integrity.

A future so bright,
a future without fright,
and love emerging from the night.

Who would have known,
one door closes and another opens.

Simile to my life,
simile to my heart,
love so grand.

I Can See The Beauty

I can see the beauty of the sun
within the days yet to come.
I can see the beauty of a full moon
within the days already passed.

I can see the beauty,
I can see the beauty.

The beauty of the sun,
the beauty of the full moon

I can see the beauty,
I can see the beauty.

Can't you too?

My Gem, She Shines, Oh Yes, She Does

My gem, she shines in the sun
oh yes, she does,
like the strikes of Lightning Alley,
she shines,
oh yes she does.

My gem, she shines in the moonlight
oh yes, she does,
like an early morning sunrise in Tokyo
she shines,
oh yes she does.

My gem, she shines in the sun
oh yes, she does,
like the gold of a Saharan illusion
she shines,
oh yes she does.

My gem she shines in the moonlight
oh yes, she does,
like Las Vegas' city delights
she shines,
oh yes she does.

Straight From The Heart

Straight from the heart,
from me to you,
I knew it from the start
that you were my type of woman.
The way we smile and laugh,
the way we talk and crack jokes,
the way we click on several levels.

Straight from the heart,
from me to you,
I knew it from the start
that you were my type of woman.
The way I feel, is so for real,
baby, it's me who wants you,
In the winter, spring, summer, and fall.

Straight from the heart,
from me to you,
I knew it from the start
that you were my type of woman,
so, here it goes,
straight from the heart,
I ask, "May I be your man?"

The man who,
loses himself in your eyes.
The man who,
you can depend on undoubtedly.
The man to,
taste the grace that rests on your lips.
The man to,
feel passion that only comes
straight from the heart.

Love's Sight

A moment's time
is what I seek,
a time in which
I pray to keep.
When your eyes met mine
for the very first time
aware was I,
of a love
definitively divine.

A moment's time
is what I seek,
a time in which
I pray to keep.
When your lips met mine
for the very first time,
my stomach stirred
as if I were a young lad
falling in love,
with love
for the very first time.

A moment's time
is what I seek
a time in which
I pray to keep.
When our best days intertwine,
when our best days are in love's sight,
we would begin to live freely
and love passionately,
learning firsthand
what love is in a moment's time
in which
I pray to keep.

JOE ADOMAVICIA

You And I Must Be

You and I must be
the ocean and sea breeze,
the softness of the sand,
or the gentle ebb and flow
of an early-morning tide.

You and I must be
the petals of a luscious red rose,
the intimacy of spring's blossom,
or gentle winds against blades of grass
of vast hills, azure bliss overhead.

You and I must be
the autumnal leaves of great oak trees,
the falling colors dancing in the air,
or a cherry blossoms pink wave
of precious and precarious relation.

You and I must be
the 'novas within ebony skies,
the vibrancy of Saturn's rings,
or the gravitational pull
of every atom within our existence,
keeping each other's love in orbit.

Elegant Continuity

It may be just me
and I may have set myself up for the kill—
but what is love without a bit of thrill?
And somewhere in my future
I see you and I,
I see your smile,
and I wonder if my words,
and I wonder if my actions,
will be the chemical reaction
that creates your joyous satisfaction.

It may be just me
and I may have set myself up for the kill—
but what is love without a bit of thrill?
And somewhere in my future
I see you and I,
I see your eyes,
and eternal love in disguise.
a gentle reminder
that a heart weld shut
has a better chance to erupt
so it's better to open up
and smile for a while.

It may be just me,
and I may have set myself up for the kill,
but what is love without a bit of thrill?
And somewhere in my future,
I see you and I,
I see our beauty in elegant continuity.

The Doors Of My Soul

If what I have seen
is what I have written,
then the beauteous blues
of the seraphic sea
are what encompass me.
And though my eyes green not blue,
you can still see the waves
ebb and flow in my eyes
entering the doors of my soul.

If what I have felt
is what I have written,
then the blood that pulsates
in my veins flows fiercely,
awakening me from within.
And although my heart is tattered and worn,
light flows through the doors of my soul
like heaven's glimmering luminosity.

If the words I have spoken
are the words I have written,
then I desire to ignite the fire
of she, whom I admire,
with words honey soaked,
and a love better lived with
than revoked.

If what I have seen,
is what I have felt,
and the words I have spoken
are the words I have written,
then the doors to my soul
remain unguarded
waiting for she who knocks
with an open heart
treasuring the warmth
of my embrace.

Prominence

If there was one thing I knew
to be true about you,
it would be the sun rises
within the iris of your eyes.
And when your gaze meets mine
I see the truest—
the divine.

If there was one thing I knew
to be true about you,
it would be the fact your touch
is able to mend the oceanic rift of reclusion
tarnishing my consciousness.

If there was one thing I knew
to be true about you,
it would be the confidence of your nature,
has will enough to enrapture
the dimness of an impending storm.

If there was one thing I knew
to be true about you,
it would be the sun sets
to the harmony of your existence—
the prominence in my world.

The Presence Of Her Excellence

The presence
of her excellence
is a gift of confidence—
Confidence that enthralls,
compels, and motivates me to be
more than I ever thought I could be.

The presence of her
excellence is a gift of integrity—
Integrity that pays forward,
a notion portraying one's true self
in the face of adversity's complexities.

The presence
of her excellence
is a gift of harmony—
Harmony that synchronizes
the two shades of the sun and moon
connecting today to tomorrow forever more.

The presence
of her excellence
is a gift of elegance—
Elegance that beautifies
my vision's perception, inceptively
More than I ever perceived could be.

Your Love Is My Faith

You are my mornings,
you are my sun,
you are my light,
and You are the reassurance
when I am hurting.
You are my afternoons,
you are my fields evergreen,
you are my flowers blooming,
and you are the wind at our backs
supporting our future.
You are my nights,
you are my moon,
you are my star,
and You are the radiance
guiding me through the night.
You are my patience,
you are my belief,
you are my trust,
and You are all the love
that fills my day with faith.

Without You

O', whatever I would do
if I were to lose you?
Roses in my eyes—
love derived.
Garden of emotion—
I'm not surprised.

O', whatever I would do
if I were to lose you?
My tears, set in motion,
quantities rivaling an ocean.

O', whatever I would do
if I were to lose you?
Though death is eventual,
my love for you,
is perpetual.

O', whatever I would do
if I were to lose you?
My mind to be lost in space,
never found again—
gone—
without a trace.

O', whatever I would do
if I were to lose you?
Instinctively and intellectually,
I'd live for you,
for, it would be the least I could do,

Beauty's Becoming (The Love We Share)

The beauty of knowing you
is beyond the glisten in your eyes,
and far beyond the amazement of you, in mine.
Before you,
fear was of abundance, and now,
life doesn't seem so bad.
The beauty of knowing you
instills me with confidence
I didn't know I had.

The beauty we see is
the beauty we become.
This truth is serene proof
we are becoming
the love we share.

The beauty of knowing you
is beyond the clouds in the sky,
and far beyond the guidance of the stars.
Before you,
my heart was jaded, and now,
the man I had a distaste for
doesn't feel so complicated,
and all of what I once felt
has no place in
the beauty
we are becoming.

The beauty we see is
the beauty we become.
This truth is serene proof
we are becoming
the love we share.

Soul On Fire

My my oh my,
you've doused my soul in gasoline,
lit the match and set my soul on fire.
I can feel it now,
don't you too?
The heat of my desire
ignited in a propensity
only for you,
whom I admire.

My my oh my,
My soul is on fire
And is hot enough to burn till my funeral pyre
The amazement of
The best blessings of life
Coming when we least expect it,
And now that I've found you
I won't let go,
No, I won't let go.

My my oh my,
you've quenched my soul
in serenity,
silenced the past,
and given me hope
in a world
more accepting
of hopelessness,
and throwing away love
as if it were expendable.

My my oh my,
I won't let go,
Now that my soul is on fire.

LOVE UNBOUND

I'm At My Happiest When I'm With You

To be frank it's quite simple,
I'm at my happiest when I'm with you.
This feeling is genuine.
You've saved me in more ways than one.
I hid in my vices,
I let crutches and insecurities encompass me and
hide me from reality only to become someone I had
no idea of and never had any desire to be.
You pulled me out of the darkness that shrouded my
mind and epitomized my everyday life.
And now the happiness that lingers through my soul
is the embodiment of belief in love I thought eluded me.
This feeling is genuine.
You saved me in more ways than one.
You embrace me for all that I am.
Until the end is where we begin.
I'm at my happiest,
when I'm with you.

Roses In The Garden

Of all the roses in the garden
I had a feeling you would be mine;
the one to soften my shell, to ease my tension.
Upon approaching you,
your aura and sensual scent lured me in one-hundred percent.
Of all the breaths of air I have taken,
I cherished the feeling of my heart
beating a bit faster around you,
and then asked myself two questions,
"How long will this drumming continue
before the rhythm would be broken and
how long until the music of my heart ceased to play?"
And without much thought thereafter
I knew what I must do.
A rose's life is ephemeral if it's not nurtured,
so I must let you bathe in the sunlight soaking up its rays,
I must nurture your roots,
I must let you be free in the wind's gentle touch
and revel when you blossom in the life of a new day.

The Key To My Serenity

There are mutual necessities
every human needs to live,
but there is one thing I need
that only you have-
and that, my dear, is your love.
A love no other
will ever feel or have as we share.
With all the people in the world there is an
equivalent amount of love to be cherished.
What I value the most about this fact
is we found each other amongst all
circumstance and possibilities.
And now I love knowing
from now till my last breath
this necessity of mine
was born in the heart of you
and is the key to my serenity.

JOE ADOMAVICIA

Mutual Fate In Oceans Of Love

She told me there were
oceans of love
within her soul,
so without question
I dove right in,
knowing
she could be my savior.
My hope is the whirlpool in mine
won't begin to drown us both.
And if by chance it does
I wonder if you will swim
for your own life
letting me drown in my own sorrows
or cling on to me
spending the seconds we have left
in our mutual fate in oceans of love.

Fearless Lover Hard Or Not At All

Praise to those who love fearlessly
Through countless rejections and failed attempts
They are those who love the hardest.
They love with passion unmatched.
They love with the soft touch of the wind,
And they love with the ferocity of a volcanic eruption.
They love, for, there is nothing else worth living for.
Praise be,
Praise be,
for those who love fearlessly.
You are those the world strives for.
Those who love hard or not at all.

Looking At You

Looking at you
is a beautiful view.
Who knew,
I'd find love so true.
O' how you know,
I'd sing a song for you
if only I could hold a tune.

Looking at you,
is a beautiful view.
Who knew,
the sky could be this blue.
O' how you know,
I'd write your name in the sky
if only I had learnt how to fly.

Looking at you
is a beautiful view.
Who knew
I'd find a soul as pure as yours,
O' how you know,
I'd travel through space
to get a glimpse of your face.

Looking at you
is a beautiful view.
Who knew
I'd find the woman of my dreams.
O' how you know,
life isn't always as it seems,
but our passion's doughty will
is everything we've ever dreamt.

My Last Sheet Of Paper

With my last sheet of paper
I thought of all the ways
I could write about you.
I knew I couldn't be too wordy
and I needed to be choosy,
but when it comes to you and I
every last metaphor and simile comes as easy as the last—
and here I speak easily of how at the end of every line
I fall off the edge of the paper
spilling my words of love in the name of you.

With my last sheet of paper
I thought of all the ways
I could write about you.
I knew I could've written in iambic pentameter
or attempted a story of a love like in the Titanic—
but you not only took a step into my heart,
you became the poetry in my life—
something no other could suffice.
And here we are, cheers, my dear,
let us live another day to write the screenplay of our life.

With my last sheet of paper
I thought of all the ways I could write about you,
and how at the end of every line
I fall off the edge of the paper
spilling my words of love
in the name of you.

AUTHOR BIO

Joseph R. Adomavicia
is a 26 year old resident of
Waterbury, Connecticut
that works at Edward Segal Inc.,
as a CNC Machinist.
At Naugatuck Valley Community College
he studies Liberal Arts and Sciences
and Mechanical Engineering.
He is a published poet,
and has been writing for 4 years.

www.ingramcontent.com/pod-product-compliance
Lightning Source LLC
Chambersburg PA
CBHW032050290426
44110CB00012B/1024